Goats

Remember Me Series

By

Caroline Norsk

Remember me I am a Goat.

Remember me I am a domestic animal.

Remember me I am smaller than the donkey.

Remember me I can also produce milk like cows.

Remember me I love to eat grass.

Remember me I am willing to eat anything even tin cans and cardboard boxes.

Remember me I can grow 2 horns.

Remember me my skin can be as furry as a sheep's skin.

Remember me I am a very curious and intelligent animal.

Remember me I can climb high places.

Remember me I maintain my balance so I couldn't fall.

Remember me I hate fences and jump over it if possible.

Remember me I live in farms, in the wilderness or in the mountains.

Remember me my name is a "kid" when I was young.

Remember me I don't like intruders.

Remember me I produce fibrous meat.

Remember me I can produce wool like a sheep.

Remember me I live in almost all continents of the world.

Remember me I speak the sound of "Me-e-e-e-eh."

Remember me I do a head butt to gain my territory.

Thank you.

Good Luck.

Made in the USA
San Bernardino, CA
01 November 2016